Praise for *The Hone*

"If you need a transfusion of love, light, and all things supplemented from Nature, then hold tight to Caroline Mellor's book of poetry, *The Honey in the Bones*. You will be transported to the crux of holy. Each word will grace your soul and send shivers to your heart. You will breathe deeper and feel the stillness you need. Like an exhale from the weight of this world, you will be touched by her transparency of being real."

—CAROLYN RIKER, Author of *My Dear, Love Hasn't Forgotten You* and *This is Love*

"Caroline Mellor is a remarkable poet, and her poems are deep and thought-provoking. She touches the chords of your heart with her authentic writing style. Her poems talk about a whirlwind of romance, darkness, light, love, and despair, and most importantly, her words are like a magic wand which pulls you out of your setbacks. Many times we try to read someone whose words stay with us even after we are done reading, that's how Caroline's work is for me. Her never-dying spirit always raises me back to my feet. This book is a product of her strength along with her powerful voice."

—GURPREET DHARIWAL, Author of *My Soul Rants: Poems of a Born Spectator* and *Kaurageously Yours*

"*The Honey in the Bones* is a collection of evocative poems that remind people to slow down, look up and connect with their senses and surroundings. Caroline Mellor's prose is honest and thought provoking with themes of nature and nurture written from the heart."

—ROXY FREEMAN, author of Times bestseller memoir, *Little Gypsy*

"Caroline's writing reveals a writer of great sensitivity and wisdom, with a gift for putting into words what she sees with her eyes and her heart. In reading her poems and stories, we discover a woman connected to nature, a loving mother who marvels at everything around her. Her texts, always poetic and hopeful, are like paintings that move us and stay with us forever. They are mirrors that reflect the beauty of the world back to you and leave you with a strong desire to embrace life and cherish the earth. Caroline's pen is a remedy for melancholy and a sweetness for the soul."

—THOMAS GAUDEX, Editor of *Scribe* and Curator of the poetry collection *The Embrace of Dawn*

The Honey in the Bones

FIRST PRINT EDITION, December 2022
FIRST EBOOK EDITION, January 2022

Copyright © 2022 by Caroline Mellor.
All rights reserved.
Set in Prata and Adobe Garamond Pro.

No part of this publication may be reproduced or transmitted in any form or by any means, electronic or otherwise, without prior written permission by the copyright owner.

ISBN: 978–1–7370545–6–6

Library of Congress Control Number: 2022952305

Printed on acid-free paper supplied by a Forest Stewardship Council-certified provider. First published in the United States of America by Golden Dragonfly Press, 2022.

www.carolinemellorwriter.com

www.goldendragonflypress.com

The Honey in the Bones

Poems to Rewild the Soul

Caroline Mellor

2022

GOLDEN DRAGONFLY PRESS

Amherst, Massachusetts

For Mathew,
Myla Rose and Sami

"The word for world is forest."
—Ursula K. Le Guin

Weald: weald \WEELD\ noun.
1: a heavily wooded area; forest.
2: a wild or uncultivated region.

Most of these poems were written in the Low Weald of East Sussex between the years of 2020 and 2022.

Contents

Winter Solstice
North
Earth

Spring Equinox
East
Air

Summer Solstice

South

Fire

Autumn Equinox
West
Water

Winter Solstice

North

Earth

Midwinter

And now
the sleeping land
calls you to rest.
Make yourself a nest
among the tangled roots;
tend the ember glow
of your soul's hearth.
Listen soft and slow
as each breath
follows the last,
with this your only task:
to dream and be dreamed
by the song of the earth
as she floats
in a black sea of stars.
Because this, my dear,
is where it all starts.
All things begin
in the sacred dark.

As the Stars Shine

I am reminded of
these truths
by the reflection
of starlight
in your eyes—

1. That the light originates
deep in the heart of a distant star
and ends light-years away
in a complex biochemical reaction
which we experience,
if we are so inclined,
as something we call
'wonder'

2. That the light travels
across vast stretches
of time and space
just to make contact
for one twinkling moment
with your moist eyeball

3. That in these days of lies
the truth is its own light;
you are a part of this great mystery
as sure as the stars shine, and
as long as the night is dark
and you are looking up,
the light will find you.

Snowdrops in December

I'm not ready for you yet—
bright and eager, out-of-place,
sharp green beaks piercing
through too-soft soil
before even autumn leaves
have turned to mud.

Let the cold hard weather come;
let the winter wrap herself around me
in a cloak of white mist
until my dreams are fully incubated.

Let the quiet flame of my soul
rest in her dark embrace,
held by the still depths
of this time outside of time.

Hold on just a bit longer,
blessed green harbingers of light.
I'll meet you above ground
in the spring. Until then,
the solace of winter
asks nothing of me,
except that I take shelter,
breathe slow, and allow
myself to be a kernel
of the deep dreaming
required by dark times.

Changing Sky

December 31, 2020

This year I saw thirteen moons wax and wane
in a changing sky. I saw the white wisp of a
comet disappear over the horizon, far out
beyond the setting sun; I saw the vapour trails
of aeroplanes vanish, replaced with the clear
blue day of a spring filled with birdsong;
I saw three hot air balloons suspended like planets
outside my bedroom window, a billionaire's
space rocket launching into the cosmos and
a lonely shower of fireworks pop and fizzle
in the black November night. I stood gawping
as Jupiter and Saturn crossed paths to become
one bright celestial light, and when I woke
on the first day of the new year, I looked up
once more and saw that the moon was still there,
white and shining, but in a different sky.

New Year's Day

Do you remember
how the sun rose gold over the forest
the first morning she was born?
It had rained for weeks.
You'd towed the caravan to our new home through fields of thick clag
  Sussex mud
while I looked on helplessly and held the cat;
we burned coal and you filled the fire engine with water from the pump
so I could have a bath.
I could hardly walk.

The night I woke you to tell you she was on her way,
you wrapped me in a brown blanket and drove me,
hot and dry-tongued through the night
to the hospital.
I remember the birth
in black and red.
I remember holding on to your legs
as though if I let go, I might not ever find my way back.
I remember the new year's fireworks
whizzing and popping outside the windows
and, hours later, holding a tiny, sweet-peach baby girl
in a clover-shaped birthing pool,
stunned with relief.
She was so calm.
Eyes bright and open, looking around
as though she'd just landed.

But most of all
I remember that sunrise.
New year's day, but it felt like spring.
You held her as I slept, a father already,

a strong and steady presence
for us to lean on.
She always was the sun rising in our skies.
You were the mountain.
And me—
I was the weather.

Before He Wakes

In the hour before he wakes,
before the traffic on the road becomes a river
and the starlight falls away into the rush,
I have already been careless and read too much of the world.
Heavy with hope and despair,
I listen to the soft rhythm of his breath.
How do I tell him,
when he asks if monsters are real,
that we are already in the jaws of an unfathomable beast?
I long to tiptoe outside now, into the blue hour,
where the crocus shoots and the birdsong are waiting
to tell me about life.
But he is stirring.
I gather him close, hold his still-dreaming head on my shoulder,
and sink back under the covers
into denial.
The day is almost light.
My thoughts give way to lunch boxes needing to be made,
and the Christmas tree needles which I should hoover
from the floor.

Imbolc

I am the dream of awakening.

I am the returning of the light.

I am the tough green shoot pushing up through the pave stones, I am the first kiss of sunlight on the unfurling petals of the snowdrop. I am the wind that whispers the gentle pull of home to the migratory bird.

I am the drop of ice melting on the mountainside with its great dream of the ocean.

I am the sap rising in the blossom tree just before it reveals its sticky buds to the sky; I am the riotous celebration humming away beneath the earth's mantle of frozen sleep.

I am the rousing of the bee from its winter slumber, and the soft pad of the mother-wolf's paw on the snow as she prepares to birth her pups.

I am hope, potential, rebirth and promise. I am the kindling breath that transforms a spark of inspiration into a blazing torch.

Give me the silent crescent moon rising over the sea and I will build you a bridge of silver light so you can walk across and lie down in it.

Give me the frost-hardened wilderness and I will breathe radiant green life over it.

Give me the healer, the poet, the craftsmith and the prophet, and I will replenish her essence and make her new again.

I am Brigid, Bast, Inanna and Hestia. I am the fierce protectress of the sacred fire.

Tonight I bestow my gifts of power and courage at the hearth of your soul. Power to shed all that which no longer serves you, and courage to clear your heart and mind for the dawn that awaits you. For I am the longing of the spirit which refuses to be consumed by a narrative of fear and chooses instead to place itself vivaciously on the side of love.

I am the song that cannot be silenced, for it is carried deep in the bones of the land. I am the flame that cannot be doused, for it is kept aglow in the hearts of the free. I am the wellspring of knowledge and the milk of the life-force. From the darkness of the earth, I give light to the fires which will forge the new world.

I am the stirring in your belly that knows what you are capable of, and just how much your gifts are needed now.

For I am the Exalted, Goddess of land, sea and sky.

I am the fire within which will not be contained any longer.

I am the quickening, I am the serpent uncoiling, I am Imbolc.

I am the dream of awakening.

Dawn

And when you first stepped out
into the pink blush of dawn
did you feel the soft, dew-soaked earth
rise to kiss your feet?
Did you notice the trees
breathe blessings down upon you
in luminous bundles of green and gold,
how every breath of woodsmoke, mist and mulch
filled your lungs like a cool river?
Did you feel yourself attached somehow
to each fading star of night
like a puppet held on threads of silver light?
And when the beautiful future
which you dreamed of so long
down that hard, broken road
finally burst over the horizon
and tumbled towards you like a wave—
were you ready to catch it?

Light

You would not
have been born
in dark times
unless your light
was needed.

Spring Equinox

East

Air

March

Winter is tired.
She longs to lie down
in the arms of spring
among the sweet
white blossoms
and the ripening buds
of new beginnings.

Go Slow

Go slow.

Go at the pace of the mosses and the trees; slow enough that green tendrils begin to sprout from your
fingernails and lichen swathes your eyebrows.

Go so slowly that your roots spread and uncoil and writhe down through soil and rock.
Be the slow medicine that this too-fast world needs.

Give yourself time to unfurl like a fern in the forest, ready to catch the sweet rain, the starlight, and the
passing butterflies.

Go gently. Remember, you have pushed through many long, hard days to get here. No wonder you are tired.

Take fallow days. They will be among your most productive times.

Wander the wild, overgrown pathways which lead to the places in you
where thousands of bright, tiny flowers open each morning to the sun
in meadows as vast as the sky.

And when the time comes to show the world your beautiful colours,
let the gentle seasons of your life work their own slow magic,
and bloom.

Plum Tree

all through winter
the tree held fast
to a single fruit

through cold and dark
and raging storms
it never snapped or fell

past ripe,
past gone,
now brown and shrunken,
like a nut-hard raisin—

now that spring
has come again
she wears it like a battle jewel
which says: I have known the darkness
and still, I blossom

Seed Moon

April 2020

It is the seed moon,
the time of sowing.
The roads and skies
have grown quiet.
Sometimes in the stillness
I can hear the earth dreaming.

There are many things I can't do
in these strange times.
But I can plant seeds.
I hold them like prayers
in the palm of my hand,
noticing their shape and size,
the way they catch the light.
Their impossible promise.
I teach my children
to make wishes on them—
and I make wishes too.

Bring nectar,
food and medicine.
Praise the sun.
Bless the wild places
and the creatures
and all those yet to come.

May this new day
be a seed itself
for the beautiful future
which wants and waits
to be born.

I think anyone who says
that miracles aren't possible
must not have planted seeds.

Fridays for Future

They may not have money
or material trappings,
property or billionaire backers,
grey-suited men in archaic corridors,
patriarchy's death throes dealing in brown envelopes;

They may just be a bunch of kids
with banners and placards and fire in their hearts
but look closer: they are a forest,
with the good green earth pushing up underneath them
and all the mountains and the rivers and the stars above them
and the ancestors and descendants spiralling outwards from them
in all directions, hand in hand, saying:

Not us
Not now
Not like this

Standing on the shoulders
of the ones who came before,
they are the beautiful future
which calls to our hearts,
for all of our children
and all of our great-grandchildren
and all our relations.

The future is a lush green forest
growing out of the wreckage.
Maybe it's time we fell in love
with it again.

Beltaine

Even the pigeons
on the spikes on top of the CCTV mast
are getting amorous

billows of cow parsley
burst from fissures
in the disused industrial estate,
all musk perfume and blousy skirts;
sassy, irresistible, intoxicating
to hapless nectar-hungry insects

dandelion suns
ripen to seed moons
which, when blown on,
erupt into orgasms of stars

in the fragments of the bluebell glade
which remain
in the central reservation of the dual carriageway,
even as the cars and trucks rush past,
at dusk, there is still a sacred hush;
holiness persists

even in the carpark
behind the shell garage
where the HGVs slumber like bison,
the impure air, heavy with petrol fumes
becomes a vessel of sex;
fragrant seeds carried on liquid seams of breeze,
intermingling with long tongues of dew-soaked grass,
green tendrils tickling, earth and sky in union,
the horned god full of lust for his sweet May bride

the moment she feels the kiss of the sun
she opens for him
like a flower

and the jagged howls of vixens a-Maying,
fucking in the hawthorn grove by the unfinished development
under a blush milk moon
would suggest that, despite the fences and the concrete mixers,
even as the last of the ancient oaks are bulldozed to make space for
more ugly houses,
the old gods here are utterly defiant,
have carnal smiles on upturned lips,
and will remain quite undeterred
in having their
wicked way.

Wild Green Magic

Before there were weeds
there were medicine beings;
healing green wonders of earth.

Before there were witches
there were wise women;
keepers of knowledge
of the ways of the forest,
speakers and listeners
of the language of the plant people.

They gathered them into their baskets
as beloved kin,
with respect and a song on their lips,
taking only what they needed.

Today, there are no
weeds in my garden,
only medicine beings.

Nettle, cleavers and dandelion,
rising up green through the cracks
in my heart.

Ground ivy, purple deadnettle, lemon balm,
restoring me to wholeness,
rewilding my tired soul.

Let my life
be an overgrown
garden:
gloriously messy,

and lightly tended
with love.

I don't know the old songs—
but if I listen carefully,
maybe the plants will trust me
enough to take me into their
wild green magic
and teach them to me.

Medicine Garden

In wild, neglected
corners of your heart
there is a medicine garden
where summer weeds
grow high as trees
and where, if you
lay down awhile
among the foxgloves
and the ferns, each flower,
each emerald leaf,
each soft-winged creature
and fleck of summer rain
will offer up its own deep song;
a light to call you home.

On Deciding Not to Try for a Third Child at Thirty-Nine

Sometimes I wonder
who you might be

a soft, sudden tug
sometimes comes over me

a whisper
in the smell of the garden
after the rain

a quiet suggestion
in the cherry blossom
as it falls

a cluster
of molecules
inside a cloud,
never quite forming
into a raindrop,
never quite landing
on the tip of my tongue
as I ponder your name

Sometimes I wonder
if your spirit
might manifest
in some other time or place:
a fresh spring daisy,
another mum's baby,
a faraway galaxy.

I don't know.
What I do know
is that there is room
in my heart for you,
bright one,
but not in my life.

So let's stay here
for just a moment,
just out of reach,
in the space between
dreaming and wonder,
on the other side of
forever.

Dandelion

All my life
I've been blown around
like a dandelion seed,
never landing long enough
to put down roots, never finding
an earthly nook of my own
to hold me while I grow
towards the sun.
All my life, I've longed
for some soft patch of green
to settle into, but I always was
floating on that high breeze,
searching—until one day
I realised that the sky
makes a fine place to live
for those with wings to fly,
and that all the ground I ever needed,
my forever home,
was you.

Gold Dust

For my children

If I could collect
all the times
you've fallen asleep
in my arms
—not just the times,
but the infinitesimal puffs
of sparkling dust
which evaporate
into the ether at
the exact moment
you slip from
the waking world
into the realm
of dreams—
I would have
enough gold dust
to colour the heavens,
enough stars to fill
the sky of my love
for you.

I Want to Grow Old With You

On Our Wedding Day

I want to grow old with you,
to see your eyes shine
though your skin grows thin
and wrinkles like paper
and your eyebrows get bushy
and your ears grow bigger.

I want to grow old with you,
to sit hand in hand on the verandah
drinking cold beers in the evening sun
looking out over the golden fields
shooting tin cans with a rusty old gun

Perhaps we'll live in the mountains
or in a house beside the sea
When the world has done with us
let's travel about in a creaky old bus
Doesn't much matter if it's you and me

I want to grow old with you,
Let's get over the hill and enjoy the view
and when the chill winds blow in
we'll always have stars
and fires in our hearts
and all the riches money can't buy will be ours
and life was a dream
spent wisely and well
for wanting to grow old with you.

Now That My Youngest Child Has Turned Three

I will miss the passing days
of soft, small hands on my heart
cherry kisses on cheeks like
moons (hers) and apples (his)
sleepy heads of spun-gold hair
heavy on my shoulder
sweet as wild honeysuckle

To My Daughter, Who Asked When She Can Join a Social Media Network

If you want to, build around yourself a coloured box
richly patterned with a camouflage of bright mosaic cubes,
which shine and move and glimmer in a thousand different hues
painting pictures of the places and the things you like to do—

But remember, these are not the story of your life.
Walls and profiles are things of two dimensions,
and you, my darling, spin whole worlds from pure light.

Don't build the walls so high the sunlight can't get in.
Resist 'branding' yourself, stay wise to your own worth.
You are more than the sum of your collected data
during your time on this one, wondrous earth.
Tend also to the cloak of woven stars
which wraps itself around your golden soul,
and the most important things, keep just for you.
Your loves, your longings, all your beautiful colours—withhold.
These things have value beyond measure;
do not be duped into giving them away to a corporation
which will reimburse you only in meaningless numbers and figures.

Remember that your light
is that of the warm sun on a fresh April morning;
you shine more brilliantly than the glow of any screen.
Take care out there, and have fun—cast free on an infinite sea,
I have no doubt that you will dream new worlds into being.

So, if you must build around yourself a box
and make use of it to share the joy you hold inside,
do not mistake it, ever, for the brighter, inner light
which, if darkness finds you, will be your surest guide.

Summer Solstice

South

Fire

A Wild Meadow Sleeps

Underneath the neat mown lawn
a wild meadow sleeps
dreaming of the day when
her colours will burst glorious
into this flower-hungry world

Moment in the Sun

Put down heavy things:
the laundry and the council tax bill,
the iPhone and the newspaper.
Put down the black and white photographs
framed in silver on the dresser
and the forgotten ideas in yellowing notebooks
which are gathering dust in the garage.
Put down that vivid, just-remembered dream
of a night twenty years ago; the strange, unnamed sadness
of an almost-memory of what might have been;
put down your hunger for adventure
and the green perspex earrings from the 80s
which your mother gave you.
Put down all the stories, all the lists and grievances,
the spoonful of sugar you could probably do without,
the stack of unread books
and the finely crafted masks you collected on your travels.
Just for now, put down the hidden bag of stones
which weighs you down—
it will still be there when you come back.
Put down your closely-guarded fears
and your dreams of a future which may or may not come,
just go outside a moment
and turn your face to the warmth
of that dazzling, golden sun.

Hedgerow

And look at you,
who they tried so hard to crop,
still donning your finest green silk gown
and joining the summer dance

Garden of Alchemy

All that mud
you threw at me?
I planted it
with flowers
and grew a
garden.

What Do You See

A note to the property developers who are
about to start building on the field down the road

Tell me, what do you see
when the June breeze brushes through the long grass
and the butterflies bob and dip and flit
from flower to flower?

Does it catch your eye
when the emperor dragonfly
patrols the grass-tops in zigzag lines,
or when the metallic green flower beetle,
slow and determined, climbs the swaying stalks
of the wild sorrel?

Do you notice the trackways left by fox and badger
and wonder for how many generations their families
might have trodden these paths?

What does it sound like, to you,
when the field hums with the song of a thousand grasshoppers
and the wood pigeon coos soft in the ash boughs
as she bids farewell to a blessed full moon night?

Can you taste it, when, after a long drought,
the first rains fall on the sun-baked meadow?
Does it not give you life, that green hay sweetness?
Is it not good?

Does the scent of the honeysuckle
and the meadowsweet in the hedgerows
not make you weak at the knees?

Do the foxgloves fail to call you, as they do me,
to vanish like a honeybee headlong into their speckled folds,
to journey down through stem and root and soil
and down through rock and crust and magma
all the way back to your own, tender heart?

How does it feel—I would like to know—
to stand and look and see all this,
to know yourself a child of this lonely, sacred earth,
to understand how rare and precious and disappearing it all is
and, before you give the signal with a flick of your wrist
to destroy it forever, to have only one thought:
"Mine"?

Winged Creatures

Be sure to leave
some parts of your soul
magnificently wild and untamed

for that is where
the winged creatures
love to visit you most

Edges

And if you feel
you don't belong,
remember that
the brightest wildflowers
always grow at the edges
of the wheat field.

Summer

Some mornings the world is drenched in gold.
Sunlight filters through the oaks in columns of mist
which land in prismic kisses on buttercup petals,
illuminating grasstop galaxies of dewdrops,
making all the field a mirrored universe of light.
Fine white clouds drift in, stretched thin on a high June breeze
as the moon daisies turn and open their bright faces to the sun.

And while some are busy telling people
it's too late, give up, go home, the gig's fucked—
the cricket chirps his prayerful song over and over,
the summer exhales a ravishment of flowers on the land,
and the blackbird, ecstatic, sings awake the millions of people
who, today, will rise and get on with creating
the blessed world which wants and waits to be born.

The Names of Wild Flowers

"Attention is the beginning of devotion."
—Mary Oliver

Find me where the rosebay willowherb grows
and the air is balmy with meadowsweet and musk mallow

Let's wander awhile through fairytale forests
of lady's slipper, gypsy weed and sweet violet

Kiss me in clouds of cornflower and cuckoo flower,
whisper secrets among the foxgloves and the flax

We'll lie in golden meadows all bejewelled with
marsh marigold, viper's bugloss and ragged robin

Before falling into dreams of enchanter's nightshade,
waking to the merry peals of fairy bells at dawn—

Meadow clary, red helleborine, yellow birds-nest:
I hold these names like incantations on the tip of my tongue,
spells to resuscitate the disappearing past.

Wood calamint, English sundew, ghost orchid:
songs of grief and longing and dreams of returning;
what beauty deadens in us when they're lost.

Lammas Blessing

Bless the earth underfoot
the breeze on my neck
the still dawn
the open sky
the feather fall
the beetle climb
the crow call
the swift fly
the cloud drift
the rising sun
the barley field
the river run
the grass seed
the ripe plum.

Bless the toad leap
the thunderclap
the kingfisher and dragonfly
the sunlight dancing on the water
the wildflowers growing in the summer
the meadowsweet
the honey bee
the blackberry moon
the gliding swan
the eyes to see
the ears to hear
are all part
of the river's song.

Bless the seed
on fertile ground
the skylark trill

the morning mist
the hazy heat
the twilight glow
the meteor shower
the midnight kiss
the fields and stones
the Lammas bread
the wheel that turns
that all are fed.

Bless us, Grain Mother
Harvest Queen
Demeter and Persephone
Sun God and John Barleycorn
All that dies shall be reborn

Bless this body
this breath
this good earth
this new day

Starlight and Tangerines

I took you both to the beach one day that summer.
We sat on the pebbles and ate crisps and tangerines;
sunlight sparkled on flowing rivulets as the tide went out
—reflections of starlight, dancing in the pull of the moon—
You dug holes in the sand, and made games of nothing much at all
and for a moment, as I sat nearby
I stared at the sea and the birds in the sky
and I thought, this must be what happiness feels like,
and I thought maybe this is how we get through all this:
by affirming the light when it lands
and by giving ourselves the grace to keep going
on the days when it doesn't.

The Butterfly Bush

I didn't plant the butterfly bush. It grew there of its own accord,
in between the apple tree and the perennial sweet peas,
an uninvited guest spiralling skywards like an exploded party popper.
It crowded out the garden path entirely, but I had not the heart
to cut it back—I enjoyed its honey fragrance too much,
the daily cohort of butterflies which arrived to sun themselves
on its purple flowering cones; sometimes five, six, even a dozen
soft-winged creatures moving meticulously across the blooms,
nectar-drunk, dipping long tongues into each sweet-scented flower
in search of ambrosia. I could stand a palm's width away
without startling them, noticing for the first time how exquisite
their wings are when seen from underneath, how they give way to hornets
but hold their own among the bees, the way they disperse
into a flurry of petals around my head if I walk past too fast.
Now the flowers are fading, but every time I pass underneath
the butterfly bush, I am reminded to move slowly, to show hospitality.
Wild and beautiful things take root in unexpected places if you let them,
and if you walk by too fast, you might scare away the butterflies.

Sweet Rain

Sweet rain falls on late summer fields;
The cloud people are sending love notes to the land.

In the garden, ripe tomatoes tumble over anarchic borders
of nasturtium, lemon balm and sweet peas; sunflowers open,
golden fennel towers tall as trees, the young apple tree stoops
under the weight of blushing fruits, plums hang poised to fall;
nature's exhalation mellows, spilling over into decay, the browning
seeds of regeneration already in place. The dream-time comes.
I sip tea and gather poems and rosemary and sage to make smudge.

Sea Song

When the chaos and haste of the human world weigh heavy
and stories of end times are all around now,
pressing down, no longer deferrable;
I go to the sea
I lose myself in the push and pull of the waves,
the salt smell,
the eternity of the sun as it bursts
into a million glittering diamonds on the surface of the water;
the breezes which wrap themselves around me,
loosening the grip of something far worse—
I stay until the light smooths a path to the horizon
and the orange orb of the sun dissolves into the sea,
I lose myself again in an ocean of twilight dreams
and at the end of that golden star-lit bridge,
I usually find me

Harvest

All summer long
the corn grows
in neat lines—
row upon row
of identical clones
sucking life from the
parched ground.
Nothing else grows.
It looks like screaming.

In August, the men come
with their machines.
They work through dusk
and into the warm night,
drowning out the Grain Moon
with the yellow glare of headlights,
the low roar of ripping and reaping.
Nothing survives the blades.
Only dust remains.

I hear the ghost
of a pristine
ancient forest
beneath the surface;
dreaming, grieving.
The world was made dead
by men at work.
Only dust remains.

Don't Tell Me

Don't tell me
about forest fires
and extinction rates
and melting glaciers

Just for today
I don't want to know

Tell me about
the scent of the meadow
as the moon rises after a hot July day
and I'll tell you
how I was watching my son eat a satsuma
and how I just got lost
in this moment of pure wonder
and then together, maybe,
we can wonder
at the universe
wondering at itself
in the guise of two human beings
talking about wonderful things

Allow me to indulge
in the privilege
of being able to switch off the bad news
which has not yet arrived at my door;
to hold my children in my arms
and hope that by some miracle
things will get better in time for them;
to remind myself that miracles
are not only possible,
but that we are walking around

inside this great miracle all the time;
that we are worlds within worlds,
impossible swirls of stardust
lighting up the sky,
made from pure love—

I want to remember
that despite it all
it is not a crime to feel happy,
and that delight
is an exalted form of resistance;
I want to walk in beauty on this earth
as my ancestors once did
as they survived plagues and wars and famines
so that I might live

So don't tell me
about forest fires
and extinction rates
and melting glaciers

Just for today
I don't want to know

Ways to Rescue Yourself From Despair

Turn towards the beauty.
Be absolutely stubborn
in your turning. Let it find you
in the way the light dances
on the surface of the river,
or in the first whispers
of the autumn as she loosens
the seed-wishes from the thistles.
Let it find you in the gentle way
an old friend wraps you
in a cloak of loving acceptance,
in the unknowable secrets of the stars
on a velvet August night, or
in the softness of the in-breath, which is
the exhalation of forests and great oceans.
Let it find you in music, poetry, prayer;
the first warm sun on your belly
after a long winter, or the way
the light falls like glass on the leaves
on a fine September day.
And when it does, hold fast.
Seize the light. Do not lend your ears
to those who bang the drums of despair;
you were not born of earth to give up.
Walk in hope, because it is your nature
and your birthright to live in joy.
When beauty finds you, breathe it in,
make a pact with it. Go gently.
And when you're ready,
create more.

Planting Trees in My Rented Garden

Planting trees in my rented garden
an apple, a plum, an ash sapling which I could not bear to destroy—
not knowing if I'll be evicted tomorrow,
not knowing if trees will be replaced with astroturf when I leave,
I felt the old familiar pang. Land, a home of my own.
A place where I could plant trees and watch them grow.

Lack.

The trees, meanwhile, reached down with spindling roots
and almost daily, or whenever I paused long enough to look,
they made their prayerful offerings –
Here: a petticoat of spring blossom,
the sound of rain on summer leaves;
Here: a charm of goldfinches on the seed feeder,
the sway and lift of branches in the evening breeze.
It would be wonderful
to plant trees in a garden of my own
and maybe watch my grandchildren climb in them someday.
But, for now, that's out of reach.
And do you know? The trees don't seem to notice.
Nor do the butterflies sunning themselves on their foliage.
I can almost see them smiling at the absurdity
of such a preposterous human idea as 'ownership'.

In this life of impermanence
why does anyone plant trees, write books, raise children?
Perhaps it is because we hope that they will grow
into something bigger than ourselves:
a great forest, with limbs stretching far up
into new skies we've not yet dreamed;
bridges to the stars, heart leaps to infinity.
An abundance of grace
which is the opposite of lack.

The Old Land

If you know where to look,
you can still find pockets of the old land:
fragments of woods in a sea of agriculture,
old flint quarries, gills and gullies,
dingley dells tucked behind industrial estates,
dew ponds and hawthorn groves where the ancient trackways intersect.
Uplands where the old ways still pulse strongly through the hills
and the land is a sleeping green Goddess.

These are the places
where the child in me goes
when I need to pray, to be with the trees.
To heal the grey, cracked places inside,
and let that old wild magic weave its way into my soul.

The first star of evening sits low over the fresh cut wheat field.
A quiet blanket of peace settles over the countryside.
This is how the land bids farewell to the summer:
with a parting message of love.

First Day

White cotton shirt,
red school jumper.
Grey shorts—age 3–4,
the age 5 ones
hung off you like a sack.
Why do I have to wear
black socks, mummy?
I don't like black,
you said. I had no answer.
I had never dressed you in black before.
It didn't match your brightness.

You had just turned four—
as other parents high-fived
and breathed sighs of relief
at the gates, all I could see
was how tiny you were.
I'd never been so unsure.

I had wanted to say, stuff this—
let's go for a picnic,
or ride a double-decker bus.
Just me, without us;
I cried on the way home.
Wish I could find some middle way
where I had you, but still had time alone.

Quiet house, empty arms, quiet tears.
Only a few more hours 'til 3.15…
the days and years go by—but today,
I'm lost without you here.

Autumn Equinox

West

Water

Nasturtium

How could I have thought you
so slow and unpromising
there among the blooming pinks of June?
When look at you now: queen of the border,
bright jewels of red, orange, and yellow,
leaves like lily pads in a fairy tale,
resplendent among the glorious mess and decay
of the autumn garden—
I would like to be more like you;
shining where all else withers

Falling Gently

When the wrongs of the world
are too much to dismantle on your own
and exhaustion settles over you like fog—

You have to
fall gently,
like a raindrop
or an autumn leaf
into the arms
of the earth
which longs
to hold you

You have to remember
that all the most beautiful things
fall down from time to time;
that all the most beautiful things
are a little broken, too.

Without You

Because I was born from your waters
and the first music I ever heard
was your heartbeat

Because the essence of you
flows through my cells like a river
and the memory of your face
is etched into my soul
the way my heart
knows the inside
of my chest

Because you were my world, once—
my earth, my first beloved home—
there can be no me
without you

and yet now,
between us,

this great forest

Lesson From an Old Tree

I went to the old grandmother oak,
a sadness sat heavy on my lungs
like a cold iron

I hoped she might have
some wisdom to impart
or at least give me the comfort
of being in the presence
of something so beautiful

I stood at her trunk
it was all gnarled and wizened
and I wondered at her age—two,
maybe three hundred years?

Does she miss the forest
which was cut down around her?
Does she feel
the rapid rate of change,
the inconsistency of the seasons
in this age of unravelling?

For many minutes I stood quietly
breathing and listening
to the sound of the rain
falling on her leaves,
hoping to hear her speak,
perhaps for some profound lesson
to filter down—

but I don't think she was listening—
she was too busy dancing
in the wind

Witches' Prayer

Great Mother,
Make me a channel of your peace.

Let my bones be the hollow chimes
through which your song flows.

Let my spirit be the still lake
that reflects your endless sky.

Let the November moon
rise whole and crimson
in the waters of my womb.

Let me fall still with the autumn leaves.
Let me dance with beauty on the descent.

Let me bury myself deep
in the dark winter earth
like a tiny seed.

Let the snow fall soft
as I sleep, sleep, sleep.

Grant me the wisdom to trust
when the time has come to emerge,
and the strength to break through
the concrete of my conditioning.

Grant me the courage to be seen,
to wear my colours with the grace
of a wildflower.

Let the morning dew gather on my petals
as I reflect the starlight of each new day.

Grant me the fearlessness
to root ever downwards and inwards
as I reach towards the sun.

So mote it be.
And it harm none.

Still

Today the harvesting of rosehips can wait.
I won't plant out the crocus bulbs
under the magnolia tree as I had planned to
or do any of the hundreds of things
which are calling out for my attention.
No: today I will sit very still in the field,
still enough for my roots to sink into the ground a little,
and for a tiny wren to hop right up to me
as though I was a sorrel stalk or a funny-looking tree.
Still enough to watch the season as it changes
and the autumn blows in on the breeze,
as I sit very still, wrapped in a blanket,
lost in a dream of falling leaves.

November

"It was November—the month of crimson sunsets, parting birds, deep, sad hymns of the sea, passionate wind-songs in the pines."
—L. M. Montgomery, *Anne of Green Gables*

Take me to the woods in November,
let's walk in the gentle peace of the trees.
Their resin smell, their dark, mushroomed trunks,
the quiet grace with which they let go their leaves.
Let's tread softly through the pinewood
over needled forest floors, which tell of secrets lost;
we'll cross the black bog on a moss-covered log
and emerge in meadows specked with galaxies of frost.
At dusk, we'll light a fire blazing skywards
and watch the sparks rise up to meet the stars,
and I'll be glad I got to walk alongside you,
my love, into winter's dream-time,
where all things are made new

On the Bridge

Here, where the ghosts of burning witches are still hunted,
one thousand years ago, when the church was built,
the river was not consulted. No one asked her if she wanted
a stone monument to an intangible god standing over her,
on sacred land which she herself had sculpted.

I wonder if she thought it strange that men should require a ceiling
to pray to their sky god in sombre, vaulted rooms, while outside,
the living world kept beating, breathing, dreaming,
whirling through her endless cosmic dance,
ancient, fluid goddess breath of healing.

Now, the floods come earlier every year.
Which is partly why, when I pass by the church and hear
a trickle of voices raised in Christian song,
I stand on the bridge and I sing to the river.
Churches come and go, but she lives on.

Alchemista

I will cast a circle
and only those with eyes to see me
will be invited in

I will take all the parts of myself
which have been deemed to be unlovable
my sensitivity
my voice
my rage
my grief
my unworthiness
my too-muchness
my not-enoughness
my loneliness

I will lay an altar
decorated with rose petals and dried sage
I will spread it with the finest Indian silk of midnight blue
and lay upon it stones of raw malachite and lapis, lace agate and tiger's eye
and wooden bowls filled with sea salt, bark of cedar, beeswax,
storm water, a red ribbon, dust,
oil of mugwort, a lock of my own hair,
a rabbit's skull and the wing of a hummingbird moth,
the golden bells which were gifted to me by the old woman on the mountain
and the small pebble which I collected from the seashore at sunrise
on the midwinter solstice

In the centre of my altar
I will place an empty bowl
deep enough to hold
all of the things
which were taken from me

and all of the shame
which I was expected to carry

I will light a fire
and dance around the flames
and the earth will be so delighted
to feel my footsteps
that my dancing will turn
lead into goose down
and poison ivy into sweet water

And when I have finished reclaiming myself
and when the last of the flames have died right down
I will pour honey and dark elderberry wine over the ashes
and I will cleanse myself with smoke and salt water
and I will watch as hyssop and wild thyme and poppies sprout
from the embers.

Failed State

There's a still, cold pause before something terrible comes
I wake in a heightened state of alarm and realise that the nightmare is real
a badger wakes from hibernation to the sound of the chainsaw and the
culling gun
a small white feather falls slowly to the ground, frozen cold and hard
as steel

Propaganda spills from petrol station news stands and television sets
there are bitter pills of rage to swallow every day, and sleeping pills
at night
a feeling that everything pure and good in this world is under threat
with hope looking less like a bright spring flower and more like a red,
squalling baby fighting for its life

Profit über alles; 'security' officers dressed in black, laughing as the ancient
trees are felled
microaggressions in supermarket aisles, on every bus and train
microaggressions without the micro, greed unchecked, humanity withheld,
my four-year-old stroking my hair, saying 'don't cry, Mama'–and ugh,
this winter rain

A dark, wet pavement with no street lamps and no umbrella
a young woman who was just walking home and a body found in the
woods a week later
a knee on the neck of an innocent man
a global pandemic crying "I can't breathe"
a feeling I can't bear this place any more—

Remembering to breathe
allowing space to grieve
remembering to believe
that change isn't just possible,
it's inevitable

One fresh morning I wake to a carrier pigeon landing on my windowsill
with a note attached to its foot, saying: 'Don't give up on me now, yours,
the future,'
while outside a blackbird is singing on the electricity pylon
and a new moon is cradling wishes in a cornflower sky—

And I remember the dreams of the night before:
a torrent bursting through a dam, bringing release.
There were a thousand prayer wheels spinning
a procession of diya oil lamps floating down a holy river
and a never ending prayer for our deliverance:

May all beings live in freedom,
may all beings awaken to the light of their true nature,
may all beings live in peace.

Temple of Tiredness

Make a temple
of your tiredness

Let it hold you
in that place
of quiet grey

Step in
to the hallowed room
which calls the
aching bones,
the heavy heart,
where the rain
on the window
sings its own
sweet melody
and a host of
feathered angels
waits to greet you

Sacred Rite

This is what I have to give:
sacral ripple of lunar tide,
blood of life, song of time,
pile of leaves, dark liquid moon,
starless river between worlds.

Scent of salt sea and gun metal,
dew-drenched moss in forest grove,
mermaid's tail, dark chocolate,
vetivert and berry-stain,
vermilion haws in autumn rain.
Burnt sage, jewelled garnet shrine,
ritual wine on a wet November night,
ripe rosehips with split ruby skins
slipped from crimson velvet lips—

Cup-full of hope and despair:
it's all there, spiralling down
into deep, delicious, heavy rest;
untamed alchemy, offered, blessed
on this mycelium prayer mat of soft black earth,
underneath a Scorpio new moon
and these wild, dancing trees.
Wind, falling leaves. Pulse of deerskin drum.
May my blood be received as a prayer of hope.
Now, let the winter come.

Mud

How
delicious
it must feel
for the leaves
when at last they let go:
the downward dance,
the fall and settle,
sweet-mulch exhalation
into Shavasana,
supine surrendering
to soft leaf-rot and
dark, fecund soil,
dissolving into
oneness with the
underworld
and all her
midnight
secrets

Sun in Sagittarius

Leave poems in supermarket car parks,
plant wildflower seeds by the side of the road.

Speak blessings on the polluted waters,
create art in ugly places.

Make your mind a secret orchard of delight.
Feast on the cherries and ripe plums.

Be shameless in your pursuit
of whatever makes your heart beat wildly.

Take rest. It is often the most radical
thing you can do.

Treat yourself with unwavering gentleness.
It will ripple outwards into the whole world.

Stage your own quiet revolution
and be prepared to be astonished at what is to come.

Let the deep light of your spirit
illuminate the way.

Things-to-Do List for Goddesses

In between
processing generational trauma
raging at profound injustice
smashing the patriarchy
paying the bills
not letting the bastards grind you down
despairing at greedy politicians
and, most likely in your spare time,
building the beautiful future
which calls to your illimitable spirit,
don't forget to feel yourself
a cosmic warrior goddess
shrouded in beauty
gifted with life
and travelling through the universe
leaving a trail of wonder
in your wake...

To the Stars

Sometimes the moon and stars
sit about my head
like an elaborate hat

Sometimes I'm sure
I have to sweep the cosmic dust
from my eyes
just to see the ordinary world

Sometimes the deep dark blue
of the mysteries
calls out to me
from far beyond the twilight

So when you tell me
to get my head out of the clouds
I will say darling, I'm way past that
I'm already halfway
to the stars

Afterwards

Afterwards,
crows were given
seats in parliament.
Growth was measured in forests,
greed was a treatable condition
and the only religion was love.
An economy based on death
was unthinkable.

We walked arm in arm
on beaches wide as skies,
our faces gold in late-day sun.
We lit fires for the ones
who had been lost
and let the great ocean tides
carry away our rivers of tears.

We talked of how the world
had never really belonged
to puffed up old men in suits,
but rather to a little girl
who planted seeds
in the soft dark earth.

We slept out beneath
a blanket of stars and
dreamed of the time before,
where we first met,
your dad and I,
in a field just after
the sunrise.

We Need to Teach the Children the Old Words

"Words are world-makers."
—Robert MacFarlane

We need to teach the children the old words,
words like brabble and grubble,
twitter-light and clinkerbell;
words which dance and trip and slip
and drip like honey off the tongue

Teach them that a hazy halo of cloud
around the moon is called a moonbroch
and that swiftly moving clouds are named cairies;
how a vixen's wedding is a sunny shower of rain,
and that a single sunbeam breaking through thick cloud
is known as a messenger

Teach them to know the seasons and scents
of queen of the meadow and bride of the sun,
how to tell Jupiter's staff from fairy fingers
and which roses bloom with the strawberry moon

Teach them to spot pricklebacks in the tottlegrass,
how to recognise a smeuse or a bishop-barnaby,
when to watch the sky for flittermice and yaffles,
and to pay attention to the dumbledore and mousearnickle
as she graces the lazy leahs of summer

Teach them a few of the old Sussex words for mud,
like gubber and slub and stodge and pug,
so they know that the precious soil beneath their toes
is anything but worthless dirt

Teach them to be users and keepers and makers
of the words which bring the land alive:
a storybook, where everything has its rightful place,
including us;
where the wilds are fearful and filled with magic
and people do noble things, and nothing is impossible

In this world of harsh new words—
words like planetary dysmorphia and solastalgia,
extinction debt and grief mitigation,
megadrought and megafire,
anthropogenic, pyrocene,
words which alarm and get stuck in our throats
describing a world which our hearts cannot grasp—
we need to teach the children the old words,
so that if they should feel lost,
the old words might colour for them
a warm and breathing, living map,
a light to guide them safely home.

We Need to Teach the Children the Old Words: GLOSSARY

brabble— to argue loudly about matters of no importance

grubble— to grope around in the dark for something that you can't see

clinkerbell— icicle

twitter-light— twilight

queen of the meadow— meadowsweet

bride of the sun— calendula

Jupiter's staff— mullein

fairy fingers— foxglove

*prickleback— hedgehog

*tottle grass— high grass

smeuse—the gap in the base of a hedge made by the regular passage of a small animal

*bishop-barnaby— ladybird

*yaffle— green woodpecker

*flittermouse— bat

*dumbledore— bumblebee

*mousearnickle— dragonfly

leah— meadow, clearing

*gubber— black mud of rotting organic matter

*pug— a kind of loam, particularly the sticky yellow Wealden clay

*stodge— thick puddingy mud

*slub— thick mud

* The words marked with an asterisk are native to my home in Sussex.

Epilogue

Sunrise Over the Field

November 2021

Morning, and the mist sits low over the field. The land is still stirring from dreams of being a forest. A thick blanket of dew has settled on the ground, illuminating a grass top city of cobwebs, and in between the blue-grey clouds, a pale, waxing moon is setting in a violet sky.

Leaves of ochre, rust and flame red drift towards the ground. Birch trees sway like underwater kelp forests. The last, yellowing leaves of the ash trees wave and flutter like fairy flags in the breeze and the oaks are clad in fine leafy crowns of burnished bronze, russet and gold: autumn's elegiac song, soon to be blown away with the coming winter winds.

When the field at the bottom of our garden came up for rent a couple of years ago, the rent was cheap, so we took it on. The previous tenant used to mow it every few weeks, keeping it flattened to a featureless stubble. Now, last year's acorns have grown into a miniature forest of saplings. Drifts of golden ragwort, birds foot trefoil and rosebay willowherb bring colour and insects in the warmer months, and many varieties of delicate, mysterious fungi grow here in the autumn. We've mown once or twice around the edges to keep the brambles from taking over, but otherwise, we let the field be.

I'm getting to know the other residents. Hobbies and buzzards, field mice and glow worms. Nettles and cleavers in the spring, elderflowers and wild roses around the summer solstice, berries and rosehips in the autumn. I gather wild foods with my children to show them how they are connected to and supported by the medicine and nourishment of the earth, and we turn our harvest into teas, soups, jams and magic potions. This is important work. We offer songs or words of thanks to the trees and plants as we forage, and have encountered emperor dragonflies, barn owls and hummingbird hawk-moths. There are sweet violets, mugwort and meadowsweet. Skeins of wild geese passing overhead on their migratory paths. Spirit made visible. A feast for the soul.

If I owned the field, I would rewild it and fall in love with it forever. Given time, I would have a young woodland to wander through. The landlady will probably mow it all down as soon as we move from here—but seeing as the field doesn't care who owns it, for as long as I am a guest of this place, I'll let the trees and wildflowers grow.

The field may not be mine, but it is part of me. When I walk barefoot in the grass, the soles of my feet absorb negative ions and trace minerals from the earth. When I breathe the air, the mushroom spores, tree pollen and sea air blown in from across the hills enter my lungs and subtly rearrange the molecular makeup of my blood. The liberty caps I find on damp autumn mornings will activate serotonin receptors in my prefrontal cortex, regenerating and igniting my neural pathways in ways that even modern neuroscience doesn't fully understand. My relationship with this plot of earth is rhizomatic. The boundaries are not clearly defined.

The exchange is more than physical. Robin Wall Kimmerer writes: "Paying attention is a form of reciprocity with the living world, receiving the gifts with open eyes and open heart."[1] In a part of the world where my ancestral wisdom has been burned, scorned and drowned out over centuries, paying close and quiet attention allows me to reclaim some part of my indigenous relationship to this place. It's an act of love and healing, a restoration of an ancient kinship, a way of relearning the language of the land, her stories and songs. For the land speaks to us in myriad ways. She guides our hearts to weave the broken threads back together.

As the field rewilds herself, she invites those parts of me which have been mown, flattened and poisoned, to come back to the fullness of life. When I offer her my presence and attention, she gifts me beauty, magic, wonder and poetry. A small red damselfly once landed on my thumb here while I was lying in the grass, daydreaming about dragonflies, as though a question was being answered. I feel safe and held by this place. I feel loved. I am home.

This winter, in fields just like this one a short way along the river from here, while the hedgehogs and badgers are sleeping in their winter dens, men will arrive with diggers and lorries and unshakeable feelings of entitlement to scrape away the precious topsoil and destroy countless habitats to make space for more ugly, unsustainable development. When

I drive or walk past these sites, I am reminded of the poet and farmer Wendell Berry's words: "There are no unsacred places; there are only sacred places, and desecrated places."[2] The land here feels what is being done to her. I share her anguish, and I fear for the creatures. A mother's first wish is to keep her children safe, to give them a safe home. When I see the current climate trajectory charts and statistics, the rate and scale of the destruction, I fear for my children too.

Lately I've been crying often, dreaming wildly, creating spontaneous rituals here and there. It's a precarious balance of hope and despair which defines this moment. The grief, the rage and the enormity of it all; the hope and vision of the young, the tenacity of the human spirit, and the prevalence of real solutions. The importance of cultivating defiant delight and human decency in the face of immense injustice. The imperative to act now. The cherishing of what beauty remains. And the feeling that nothing else matters, nothing at all.

In all this chaos and confusion, I seek strength in the ancient truth that all things move in cycles, and all things change in time. While I'm grappling as best as I can with the facts, I am also a mother. Mine is a desperate hope. My heart refuses to accept the grim and apocalyptic story that humankind is simply doomed – and as dire as the outlook may seem, the agency of the times in which we live has perhaps never been greater.

The field is a portal to that which mythologist and storyteller, Dr. Martin Shaw, calls "our old, ancient, primordial Beloved, which is the Earth herself."[3] It is a microcosm of a planet where everything is living and connected, where spirit speaks in the language of beauty. A reminder that the plan here on earth, even in this age of death, is life, and that life, against inconceivably improbable odds, tends to be quite good at finding a way.

When I feel overwhelmed, it is often a good idea to get my hands in the soil, to go to ground. These are dark, uncertain times—but the dark is home to fertile, regenerative magic, which Rebecca Solnit refers to in her seminal book, *Hope in the Dark,* as a "darkness as much of the womb as the grave."[4] And when darkness gathers, it's time to plant bulbs.

Later that same November day, I will take a sack of crocus bulbs and plant them beside the bridge which connects the garden to the field. Each bulb is an act of faith, an offering to life and the future, an embodiment of reciprocity, and a promise to the coming spring. When the flowers appear in early spring in bright bursts of purple, white and gold, I will welcome the return of the light, and give thanks that we made it through.

Autumn leaves dance around me and float down towards the ground, into the waiting arms of winter's rest. I finish my tea; the kids will soon be up. A bright green woodpecker flashes through the trees. Calls of blackbird, robin and wren infuse the air with song, and meandering trackways left by fox and badger snake through the long grass, betraying the secrets of the night before.

I don't have any answers. As we stand at the crossroads of the "no longer and the not yet,"[5] perhaps the true magic of this liminal moment lies in our ability to navigate uncertainty with the courage to hope, and to act, and to dare to believe that our story can still be a beautiful one. To plant the bulbs, dream fresh dreams, and trust that spring will come.

I breathe deep. A soft, earthy taste of mulch coats my tongue with a cool, metallic tang. A sparrowhawk swoops low over the field and then disappears over the hedgerows, away into the light of the rising sun.

[1] Kimmerer, Robin Wall. *Braiding Sweetgrass: Indigenous Wisdom, Scientific Knowledge and the Teachings of Plants*. Milkweed Editions, 2013.

[2] Berry, Wendell. *Given: Poems*. Counterpoint LLC, 2005.

[3] Shaw, Martin. *Mud and Antler Bone*, Emergence Magazine, Inverness CA, 2018.

[4] Solnit, Rebecca. *Hope in the Dark: Untold Histories, Wild Possibilities*. Haymarket Books, 2016.

[5] Escobar, Arturo. *Thinking-feeling with the Earth: Territorial Struggles and the Ontological Dimension of the Epistemologies of the South*, aibr.org, 2015.

Acknowledgements

There is usually only one name on the cover of a book, but a book is truly a whole ecosystem.

Firstly, thank you to all at Golden Dragonfly Press, especially to Alice Maldonado for her insight and editorial support.

I owe a debt of gratitude to Robert Macfarlane for graciously allowing me to use his words as the epigraph and inspiration for the poem 'We Need to Teach the Children the Old Words,' and for telling me not to change the name of the book.

Thanks is also owed to the editorial teams at Medium, Rebelle Society, and Women's Spiritual Poetry, where many of these poems or earlier versions of them were first published.

Heartfelt thanks to Anna Hope and Roxy Lepron for early readings, and for affording me the great kindness of writing some words of praise for the cover. I'm honoured!

I am deeply grateful to Thomas Gaudex, Editor of Scribe, for his ongoing support and confidence in me.

A huge thank you to my unofficial, virtual Medium writer's circle for their feedback and words of wisdom and encouragement. Notably, but not restricted to John O'Neill, Jenine Bsharah Baines, William Spirdione, Franco Amati, Connie Song, Michelle Berry, Sally Mortemore and Deborah Barchi, and especially to Carolyn Riker, Gurpreet Dhariwhal and Thomas Gaudex, who also contributed endorsements for this collection. I'm thankful to have you all on my team!

Thank you to Clementine Wilson for professional photography for the book cover.

I'm grateful to my friend Jelly Juleida for allowing me to use her words as the first line of 'We Need to Teach the Children the Old Words.'

Thank you to my friends: the mothers, healers, artists, music makers, dreamers, carers, teachers, activists, field gravitators, gentle world creators and protectors; those who, every day, in a myriad of ways both loud and quiet, make their lives mean love. And to the incredible young people who give me so much hope: thanks and blessings. The future is yours!

Thanks especially to all those who have, over the years, been supportive of my writing efforts, namely Emer Mary Morris, Ewen Lappin-Cook, Mark Charlton, Polly Eason & tribe, Leigh Dowsett, Silvia Lopez, Gemma Challenger, Gemma Allan, Melissa Corkhill and Rainbow Auntie Alison Dowell. I'm grateful for your kindness.

A deep bow of gratitude and respect to the spirits of the land, the rivers, the trees and the plant beings who have blessed me with their beauty and inspiration.

To my grandmother Joyce Dowell, and to all those who came before.

To my parents, Kate and Derek. I love you.

To the great many teachers and elders who speak to me from my bookshelves.

To Maddy Elruna for telling me to go for it.

To anyone I've forgotten who deserves to be thanked.

Endless love and gratitude to my beautiful children, Myla Rose and Sami, who all of this is for.

Lastly, and mostly, thank you to my husband Mathew Bulba for his constant love, support and unwavering enthusiasm. Without him this book would indisputably not have been written. To him and anyone else who has done me the honour of reading these words: may all your wildest dreams come true. The world needs them.

Caroline Mellor, August 2022

Printed in Great Britain
by Amazon